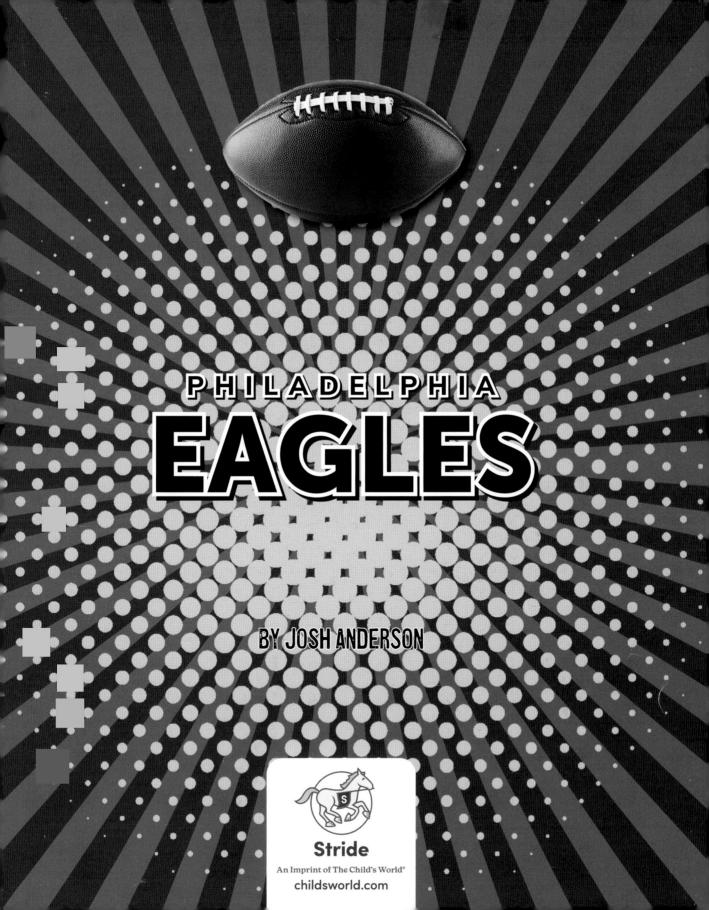

PHILADELPHIA
EAGLES

BY JOSH ANDERSON

Stride

An Imprint of The Child's World®
childsworld.com

The Child's World®
childsworld.com

Published by The Child's World®
800-599-READ • www.childsworld.com

Photography Credits
Cover: © Mitchell Leff / Stringer / Getty Images; page 1: © Africa Studio / Shutterstock; page 3: © Grant Halverson / Stringer / Getty Images; page 5: © Todd Kirkland / Stringer / Getty Images; page 6: © Tony Duffy / Staff / Getty Images; page 9: © Patrick Smith / Staff / Getty Images; page 10: © Mitchell Leff / Stringer / Getty Images; page 11: © stevezmina1 / Getty Images; page 12: © Kevin C. Cox / Staff / Getty Images; page 12: © Mitchell Leff / Stringer / Getty Images; page 13: © Jonathan Daniel / Stringer / Getty Images; page 13: © Mike Ehrmann / Stringer / Getty Images; page 14: © Elsa / Staff / Getty Images; page 15: © Streeter Lecka / Stringer / Getty Images; page 16: © Everett Collection / Newscom; page 16: © Otto Greule Jr / Stringer / Getty Images; page 17: © Brian Killian / Stringer / Getty Images; page 17: © Jonathan Daniel / Staff / Getty Images; page 18: © John Booty / Flickr; page 18: © PhillyPartTwo / Wikimedia; page 19: © Harry How / Staff / Getty Images; page 19: © Gregory Shamus / Staff / Getty Images; page 20: © Christian Petersen / Staff / Getty Images; page 20: © Mitchell Leff / Stringer / Getty Images; page 21: © Rob Carr / Staff / Getty Images; page 21: © Kevin C. Cox / Staff / Getty Images; page 22: © Rob Tringali / SportsChrome / Newscom; page 23: © Nick Laham / Staff / Getty Images; page 23: © stevezmina1 / Getty Images; page 25: © Andy Lyons / Staff / Getty Images; page 26: © Ezra Shaw / Staff / Getty Images; page 29: © Jim McIsaac / Stringer / Getty Images

ISBN Information
9781503857834 (Reinforced Library Binding)
9781503860636 (Portable Document Format)
9781503861992 (Online Multi-user eBook)
9781503863354 (Electronic Publication)

LCCN 2021952638

Printed in the United States of America

TABLE OF CONTENTS

GO EAGLES!

The Philadelphia Eagles compete in the National Football **League's** (NFL) National Football Conference (NFC). They play in the NFC East **division**, along with the Dallas Cowboys, New York Giants, and the Washington Commanders. The division is known for having some of the oldest rivalries in all of football! And Eagles fans are known for being very passionate about "the Birds," one of their nicknames for the team. Let's learn more about the Eagles!

NFC EAST DIVISION

| Dallas Cowboys | New York Giants | Philadelphia Eagles | Washington Commanders |

IT'S ALWAYS A BIG GAME WHEN THE EAGLES FACE OFF AGAINST A RIVAL FROM THE NFC EAST.

BECOMING THE EAGLES

The Eagles joined the NFL as an **expansion team** in 1933. That's the same year President Franklin D. Roosevelt created the National Recovery Administration (NRA). The NRA's goal was to help Americans during the Great Depression. The NRA's symbol was an eagle, which inspired the Philadelphia owners to call their team the Eagles. The Eagles played in three-straight NFL Championship Games from 1947 to 1949, winning two of them. They won the NFL Championship again in 1960.

RON "JAWS" JAWORSKI (CENTER) WAS THE EAGLES' QUARTERBACK FOR TEN SEASONS IN THE 1970S AND 1980S.

BY THE NUMBERS

The Eagles have won **ONE** Super Bowl.

15 division titles for the Eagles

474 points scored by the team in 2014—an Eagles record!

13 wins for the team in 2017

THE EAGLES APPEARED IN THE BIG GAME TWO OTHER TIMES BEFORE FINALLY WINNING SUPER BOWL 52.

WHEN JETS SOAR ABOVE A SPORTING EVENT, IT'S CALLED A FLYOVER.

The Eagles play their home games at Lincoln Financial Field, also known as "The Linc." Before the team moved into The Linc in 2003, they played for more than 30 seasons at Veterans **Stadium**. The Eagles share The Linc with the Temple University Owls football team. On game days, around 68,000 fans can fit inside the stadium to cheer for Philadelphia. The Eagles have hosted three NFC Championship Games at The Linc.

We're Famous!

Vince Papale was a wide receiver for the Eagles from 1976 to 1978. He was the subject of the 2006 movie *Invincible*. Actor Mark Wahlberg portrays Papale in the film. Papale never played college football. The movie tells the inspirational story of how he earned a spot on the Eagles' roster as a 30-year-old **rookie**.

GREEN

WHITE

Truly Weird

A 1988 playoff game between the Eagles and Chicago Bears was nicknamed the "Fog Bowl." According to people at the game at Chicago's Soldier Field, the fog was so thick on the field, it was like having clouds on the ground. This happened because cold air over Lake Michigan mixed with warm air at Soldier Field. Players on the field couldn't see more than a few yards in front of them. The Eagles lost 20–12.

Alternate Jersey

Sometimes teams wear an alternate jersey that is different from their home and away jerseys. It might be a bright color or have a unique theme. The Eagles wore their kelly green "throwback" uniforms during the opening game of the 2010 season against the Green Bay Packers. The new look proved unlucky, though. The Eagles lost 27–20.

EAGLES PLAYERS RUN THROUGH A CLOUD OF SMOKE DURING INTRODUCTIONS AT LINCOLN FINANCIAL FIELD.

TEAM SPIRIT

Going to a game at The Linc can be a blast! After every Eagles **touchdown**, the crowd sings along to the team's fight song, "Fly Eagles Fly." It's one of the best-known fight songs in the NFL! The Philadelphia Eagles Cheerleaders entertain fans during breaks in the action. Joining the cheerleaders to pump up the crowd is Swoop, a giant costumed bald eagle. Swoop is known for crazy stunts like zip-lining across the field or parachuting into the stadium! Hungry fans at The Linc can enjoy a Philly cheesesteak from Tony Luke's.

SWOOP

HEROES OF HISTORY

Chuck Bednarik
Center/Linebacker | 1949–1962

Most players in the league play offense or defense. Bednarik played on both sides of the ball. One of the fiercest tacklers in the league, he was selected for the Pro Bowl eight times. Bednarik is a member of the Pro Football **Hall of Fame**.

Randall Cunningham
Quarterback | 1985–1995

Cunningham was one of the earliest "dual-threat" quarterbacks. That means he could help the team by throwing the football or running with it. Cunningham's 4,928 rushing yards rank third all-time for a quarterback. He led the Eagles to 63 victories as the team's starting quarterback.

16

Brian Dawkins
Safety | 1996–2008

Dawkins is the only player in NFL history to record a **sack**, intercept a pass, recover a fumble, and score a touchdown in the same game. He had 911 solo tackles in his career. Dawkins was chosen for nine Pro Bowls and is a member of the Pro Football Hall of Fame.

Donovan McNabb
Quarterback | 1999–2009

McNabb is the Eagles all-time leader with 32,873 passing yards and 216 passing touchdowns. He led the Eagles to the **playoffs** in eight of his seasons with the team. The team won 92 games with McNabb as their quarterback. He was chosen for six Pro Bowls.

DECEMBER 26, 1960

The Eagles defeat the Green Bay Packers in the NFL Championship Game. It's the only postseason loss ever for Packers coach Vince Lombardi.

The Eagles defeat the Dallas Cowboys in the NFC Championship Game 20–7. They advance to play in Super Bowl 15.

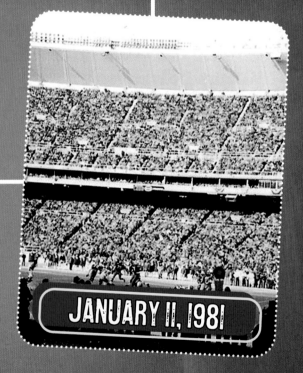

JANUARY 11, 1981

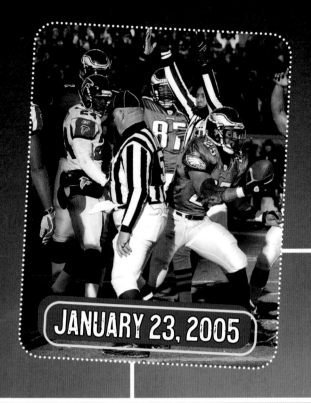

JANUARY 23, 2005

By defeating the Atlanta Falcons 27–10 the Eagles advance to play in Super Bowl 39 against the New England Patriots.

The Eagles select University of Alabama wide receiver DeVonta Smith with the tenth pick in the first round of the NFL Draft.

APRIL 29, 2021

MODERN-DAY MARVELS

Fletcher Cox
Defensive Tackle | Debut: 2012

Cox was selected for six-straight Pro Bowls from 2015 to 2020. That's one short of an Eagles record. Through the 2021 season, his 58 sacks are the most ever by an Eagles defensive tackle. Cox was honored with a selection to the NFL's 2010s All-Decade Team.

Jalen Hurts
Quarterback | Debut: 2020

After a record-breaking college career, Hurts was selected by the Eagles in the second round of the 2020 NFL Draft. He started four games as a rookie. In a game against the Arizona Cardinals, he tied the Eagles rookie record by throwing three touchdown passes. Hurts led the team to the playoffs in 2021.

Jason Kelce
Center | Debut: 2011

From his rookie year through the 2021 season, Kelce started in every game he played for the Eagles. He's been chosen for the Pro Bowl five times. Kelce was a key part of the Eagles' team that won Super Bowl 52.

DeVonta Smith
Wide Receiver | Debut: 2021

In 2020, Smith won the Heisman Trophy award, given to college football's best player. After his incredible career at the University of Alabama, the Eagles picked Smith tenth overall in the 2021 NFL Draft. He scored a touchdown in his first NFL game! Smith finished his rookie season with 916 yards receiving and five touchdowns.

THE EAGLES RETIRED
REGGIE WHITE'S NUMBER 92
JERSEY IN 2005.

REGGIE WHITE

White ranks second all-time with 198 career sacks. Nicknamed "The Minister of Defense," he forced 33 fumbles during his career and combined on 1,111 tackles. White was picked for the Pro Bowl 13 seasons in a row. He was chosen two times as the NFL's Defensive Player of the Year. White was honored with induction into the Pro Football Hall of Fame in 2006.

FAN FAVORITE

Brian Westbrook–Running Back
2002–2009

During his eight seasons with the Eagles, Westbrook totaled 9,785 yards rushing and receiving. Barely over 200 pounds, he was beloved by Eagles fans for the way he used his speed and agility to avoid tacklers. He was a key part of the 2004 Eagles team that advanced to play in the Super Bowl.

#1

THE BIG GAME

FEBRUARY 4, 2018 – SUPER BOWL 52

Quarterback Carson Wentz led the Eagles to an 11–2 record to start the 2017 season. Then he suffered an injury that ended his season. Many fans thought the Eagles' chance for a championship was over. But backup quarterback Nick Foles led the Eagles to playoff victories over the Atlanta Falcons and Minnesota Vikings. Then the Eagles entered Super Bowl 52 as underdogs to the New England Patriots. In the big game, Foles threw three touchdown passes and earned the Most Valuable Player award. The Eagles won the game, 41–33.

ALSHON JEFFREY'S (LEFT) FIRST-QUARTER TOUCHDOWN CATCH GAVE THE EAGLES THEIR FIRST LEAD OF SUPER BOWL 52.

ANDY REID LED THE EAGLES TO 130 REGULAR SEASON VICTORIES.

AMASING FEATS

4,039
Passing Yards

In 2019 by
QUARTERBACK
Carson Wentz

17
Rushing
Touchdowns

In 2011 by
**RUNNING
BACK**
LeSean McCoy

116
Catches

In 2018 for
**TIGHT
END**
Zach Ertz

35
Field Goals

In 2016 for
KICKER
Caleb Sturgis

ALL-TIME BEST

PASSING YARDS

Donovan McNabb
32,873

Ron Jaworski
26,963

Randall Cunningham
22,877

RUSHING YARDS

LeSean McCoy
6,792

Wilbert Montgomery
6,538

Brian Westbrook
5,995

RECEIVING YARDS

Harold Carmichael
8,978

Pete Retzlaff
7,412

DeSean Jackson
6,512

SACKS**

Reggie White
124

Trent Cole
85.5

Clyde Simmons
76

SCORING

David Akers
1,323

Bobby Walston
881

Jake Elliot
529*

INTERCEPTIONS

Eric Allen
34

Bill Bradley
34

Brian Dawkins
34

*as of 2021
**unofficial before 1982

LESEAN MCCOY LED THE NFL WITH 1,607 RUSHING YARDS IN 2013.

GLOSSARY

division (dih-VIZSH-un): a group of teams within the NFL that play each other more frequently and compete for the best record

expansion team (EK-span-shun TEEM): a new team added to the league

Hall of Fame (HAHL of FAYM): a museum in Canton, Ohio, that honors the best players in NFL history

league (LEEG): an organization of sports teams that compete against each other

playoffs (PLAY-ahfs): a series of games played after the regular season that decides which two teams play in the Super Bowl

Pro Bowl (PRO BOWL): the NFL's All-Star game where the best players in the league compete

rookie (RUH-kee): a player playing in his first season

sack (SAK): when a quarterback is tackled behind the line of scrimmage before he can throw the ball

stadium (STAY-dee-um): a building with a field and seats for fans where teams play

Super Bowl (SOO-puhr BOWL): the championship game of the NFL, played between the winners of the AFC and NFC

touchdown (TUTCH-down): a play in which the ball is brought into the other team's end zone, resulting in six points

FIND OUT MORE

IN THE LIBRARY

Bulgar, Beth and Mark Bechtel. *My First Book of Football.*
New York, NY: Time Inc. Books, 2015.

Jacobs, Greg. *The Everything Kids' Football Book, 7th Edition*.
Avon, MA: Adams Media, 2021.

Sports Illustrated Kids. *The Greatest Football Teams of All Time*.
New York, NY: Time Inc. Books, 2018.

Wyner, Zach. *Philadelphia Eagles*. New York: AV2 Books, 2020.

ON THE WEB

Visit our website for links about the Philadelphia Eagles:
childsworld.com/links

Note to parents, teachers, and librarians: We routinely verify our web
links to make sure they are safe and active sites. Encourage your
readers to check them out!

INDEX

ABOUT THE AUTHOR

Josh Anderson has published over 50 books for children and young adults. His two boys are the greatest joys in his life. Hobbies include coaching his sons in youth basketball, no-holds-barred games of Apples to Apples, and taking long family walks. His favorite NFL team is a secret he'll never share!